The Five Star Plan

Replacing Politicians with Patriots

Robert West

In Memory of

Justice David Bridges

"He has told you, O man, what is good; and what does the Lord require of you but to do justice, and to love kindness, and to walk humbly with your God?"

Micah 6:8

The Five Star Plan
Copyright © 2021 Robert West

Interior: Robert West
Cover Design: Carole West
Photography: Rick Parent
ISB: 9798582662259

Contents

Forward

How has America devolved to the point where the overwhelming majority of the people do not like and do not trust government at any level? The answer is quite simple. The government we get is the government we elect, and the government we continue to have is that which we tolerate. Edmund Burk predicted this when he said, "All that is necessary for evil to triumph [is] for good men to do nothing."

Unfortunately, we Americans have abdicated the responsibilities that are required of a self-governing society. In his Gettysburg address, Lincoln borrowed a phrase from John Wycliff when he spoke of "... government of the people, by the people and for the people."

Today, I would say that the government we have is a result of the failure of the American people to responsibly participate in the process of selecting governing officials at all levels of government from the school board to the city, county, state, and federal. A lack of good vetting has too often resulted in the election of people who should never be allowed to make governing decisions. And, after election, the failure of the people to follow, analyze, and report on the actions and votes taken once the person is in office has resulted in the continuous reelection of people who say one thing when campaigning and often do just the opposite, or at least less than the campaign rhetoric.

"Of the people, by the people, and for the people" is not just a cute statement; it is foundational to the survival of our constitutional republic form of government. George Washington said, "Bad officials are elected by good citizens who do not vote."

If we Americans are to have a government that serves the people, we must become more involved in electing, watching, and holding elected officials accountable for their actions in office.

Robert West's book, "The Five Star Plan" lays out in clear, specific detail how "we the people" can regain our role in ensuring that our founding fathers' brilliant plan for life, liberty, and the individual pursuit of happiness can be rescued from the dominating hand of the socialist democrats who now control too many states and our nation. "The Five Star Plan" is a must- read for every constitutional conservative with Judeo-Christian values.

But most important of all, it is not a book just to be read. It presents a plan that must be acted upon or Ronald Reagan's prediction that "Freedom is never more than one generation away from extinction. We didn't pass it to our children in the bloodstream. It must be fought for, protected, and handed on for them to do the same, or one day we will spend our sunset years telling our children and our children's children what it was once like in the United States where men were free," will come true.

We must end the apathy that got us here and begin the action presented by Robert West. We owe it to those who sacrificed their lives to protect our nation, and we owe it to future generations.

Texas Senator, Bob Hall

1

The Beginning

At the start of 2020 my wife and I attended a family event in Houston and by the time we returned home, we contracted Covid-19. We were sick for a few days with a fever and tired several days afterward. It would be weeks before we would know this odd flu, we experienced had a name or that it would become a world-wide event in 2020.

Then during the early stages of the pandemic, I travelled across North Texas in an attempt to represent Texas Congressional District 4 in Washington D.C. It may sound odd but I did not want to be a congressman as much as I wanted to serve as one. When I started the people stepping forward were either not living in the district or most of them were from the same town as the last three representatives. That made up 60 plus years of one area having a congressman in a district that stretched from the outskirts of Dallas to the eastern border of Texas. I remember speaking to a group near the border telling them, "you haven't been forgotten, you haven't even been discovered." It sounds harsh, but it was true.

Along the way my wife and I became delegates to the first virtual Texas Republican State Convention. We were blessed to have met several great people during this time. To name a few, Judge David Bridges, Col. Allen West, Cat Parks, Senator Bob Hall, Justice Mark Russo, 18 County Chairs, 150 or so Precinct Chairs and almost twenty candidates for the same position I was seeking.

When the selection process was complete, I had lost and was somewhat relieved. I foolishly thought I could go back to being the guy that worked on airplanes and developed land.

A few months later my wife and I attended an "Open Up Texas" rally in Austin where a few of those people were guest speakers. It was a peaceful event in front of the governor's mansion and no, Abbott didn't show up.

Afterwards, I started reaching out to others by bringing attention to the worst of Governor Greg Abbott's abuses. I found that short of five senate and house members, nobody was standing up to him openly, not even democrats. However, the Texas Republican GOP Executive Committee had voted 58-4 to criticize the governor. This overwhelming vote by the Texas State Republican Party against a sitting governor from their own party shows just how far Abbott had gone by that time.

I went through the Texas Constitution and it was clearly being violated by the present governor. Beginning with, the government will never close Texas beaches to the public and Abbott had done that. The law also sets the election dates and they cannot be changed without legislative approval and Abbott changed them.

One person, Greg Abbott, decided what businesses were "essential" and what businesses were "non-essential" and just like that, destroyed a state's booming economy and put millions of people out of work for months.

Greg Abbott had closed the hospitals to people without Covid-19, including people that needed chemotherapy. People died and not just from Covid-19. No massive number of Covid-19 patients appeared and hospitals laid off staff, closed entire wings and in one case a hospital in Houston went out of business. The state lost hospital capacity not due to being overrun with patients but for lack of patients.

On top of that, the hospitals would receive additional money for admitting critically ill Covid-19 patients but not for keeping people from getting ill. The hospitals did not treat people with mild symptoms but sent them home until they were sick enough to admit. We treated no other illness like this until then. We've never sent home stage one cancer patients and told them to come back when they reached stage four. So, why had this become standard practice during a pandemic?

For all of these reasons and more Texans asked our State Representatives and Senators to reign in Abbott, to threaten him with impeachment if he refused but it fell on deaf ears. Even Democrats would not challenge Abbott and so, for too many months, one person ruled Texas by decree.

Abbott was trying everything he could to reward his supporters. Very close to the election, too late to do any real good, he made large financial donations to their campaigns. President Trump had talked about draining the swamp but the swamp was at my doorstep, not the city limits of D.C. The swamp included Blue and Red creatures but what could I do?

Well folks, with the help and advice from a lot of smart people and an optimism you think would have dimmed by now, I set out to change things. What you are reading now is my best hope to do just that.

This book explains what you can do, it reminds the people that you are the public and the office holders are the servants. Why and when we began treating our servants as something above us instead of the other way around is not important. What is vital now, that starting today you have permission to say to any official, including the President of the United States, "Me Public, You Servant." It helps if you use a Tarzan voice.

I will try to the best of my abilities to spell out what we need to accomplish to change things right now and for generations to come.

If you are looking for a rah-rah book about the Republican Party or the state of Texas look elsewhere. As of November 2020, I believe the Republican Party of Texas has all the right people in leadership and very few of the right people in office. As for Texas, if you love it as much as I do it just seems cruel to brag.

The Five Star Plan is about replacing every Texas politician that did not stand up to Abbott, with citizen-legislators. This begins at the county all the way up to the state level. This is the drive for our tagline, Replacing Politicians with Patriots. While we're at it, let's go ahead and replace every career politician that didn't challenge the Federal Election of 2020 that was an unconstitutional nightmare.

How do we do this impossible task you ask? In 2022 the great state of Texas will have their Primary Elections. Every state office holder will be looking to get reelected or elected and that is your one true chance to make a difference. Not the General Election, but the Primary Election that too many people skip.

Texas voters turn out for Presidential Elections, but not so much for off year elections. If you look at the numbers, you'll notice they hardly bother with local elections. When the 2018 Primaries happened, only a million and a half Texans participated in the process. That Primary vote decides whose name will go under the Republican slot for Governor, Texas Senators and our Texas State Representatives. That vote will also decide many County elected positions.

When it gets to the General Election in 2022 if the choice is between Abbott and a Democrat you might hold your nose and vote for Abbott again. You might not vote at all or maybe you'll just pull the lever for a Democrat because of what Abbott has done to Texas.

In any event, I think whoever runs under the Texas Republican banner will win, so we need to make sure the right person gets that honor.

How do we do that? The goal is to add three and a half million more voters to the 2022 Texas Republican Primary. A million primary voters for each point of the Texas Star and at least 3 of those pointing to the exit for career politicians that cared more about their career than the voters or the constitution they swore to uphold.

It may sound a bit old-fashioned but I believe when a person takes an oath before God and the people, they should hold themselves to it.

My guess is about half a million regular Republican Primary voters will back anyone other than Abbott in the Primary Elections. Either over his excesses or for fear of losing the governor's mansion to the Democrats. These establishment Republican voters will be on our side.

We know that more than half of Texans pray daily and almost 70% profess a strong belief in GOD. These people had their churches shut down for months. The mandates and decrees might have come from Greg Abbott but most of the Texas House and Senate members did nothing to stop them. Those that stood against Abbott will be invited to be part of our project, those that sided with Abbott are not invited.

Bars were also shut down during this time so there is another group of Texans upset that we can ask to join in this effort. Add in small business owners and that is a LOT of Texans, millions of Texans, a vast majority of Texans.

Our state has one church for each 2,000 people and one bar for each 10,000 people. In Texas some of these people will go into a bar but never a church, some will go into a church but never a bar. There are few people in Texas that will not go into either.

The Texas Five Star Plan calls for five million voters to participate in the Republican Primary Election of 2022. It calls for you to recruit five people, educate them and get them to vote in the 2022 Republican Primary. This plan also calls for our newly elected citizen legislators to pass five items before anything else and to stop everything else until or unless these things get made into law.

If you've never voted in a Primary Election, especially the Republican Primary and if your friends and family have never voted in one before, try it this time and see what can happen.

We know people are busy, money is tight and politics has gotten to the point of voting for the lesser of two evils. I for one am tired of voting for evil and will no longer do it.

You are the public, they are the servants, and it is time to remind them of that. If you want to run for office or know someone that would make a good representative, we need candidates. You have this step by step book to guide the way and the

TFSP website offers additional resources. None of these work without you.

If you think politics is not for you, think again. Your work and taxes keep it all moving and if you are going to be forced to pay for the band you sure ought to have a say in choosing the music.

Many elected officials in Texas say we should never push Republican ideas because we would be encouraging a rule by the majority. Of course, we support this, if you don't have the majority rule that only leaves one option, minority rule.

I will answer your questions and point the way. Welcome to the team and take pride in being a Texas Five Star Patriot.

The Beginning Summary

✓ We are the Public; you are the Servant.

✓ The Five Star Plan begins with every Texas politician that did not stand up to Abbott.

✓ TFSP calls for five million voters to participate in the Republican Primary Elections of 2022.

✓ We need Five Star Patriot candidates.

2

The Five Star Agenda

The Five Star Plan begins with real ambition and calls for voting in the 2022 Republican Primary Election.

The first thing you might say to voting in a Republican Primary is that, "you don't see yourself as a Republican" and that is fine. Texas has open Primaries and you can still vote in the Republican Primary even if you're not involved or may be involved with another conservative group. You cannot vote in both the Democrat and Republican Primaries but you can vote in either.

Many people think since they're not active in the Republican party they should not vote in these elections. That mindset is bad because the primary vote decides the party candidate for office. Primary Elections often have several options but once they are narrowed down then you only have two, a Republican and a Democrat.

Why would a "regular voter" want to vote in a Republican Primary Election? Across most of Texas from the senate on down to dog catcher a Republican holds the majority of these positions. Since these people are going to end up getting elected anyway, why not have a say in which one gets elected?

When the general election arrives, you can still vote for whoever you want on either side. For someone living in a poor area of Dallas, they might vote straight Democrat. Those same voters also know they need a gun to protect their family. By voting for a Five Star candidate just one time could very well ensure that better gun laws would be easier to pass in a legislation session.

Let's talk about our legislative agenda. This section is up front because you need to determine if you want to be involved in this plan. We have our top five points set for the first legislative agenda. To be a TFS each candidate must agree and vote for this agenda. If they vote against any of these points they will be booted, no ifs, ands or buts about it. For legislatures who don't comply, they will have already upset the establishment; they will have no organization to support them if they wish to continue serving in public office.

FIVE STAR LEGISLATIVE AGENDA

1. **TEXAS GOVERNOR EMERGENCY POWER ELIMINATED**: It was never within the legislature's ability to pass the law according to the Texas Constitution. The Texas Legislature can no more grant the governor powers the constitution does not grant him than they can take the powers the constitution gives him.

2. **CONSTITUIONAL CARRY**: The U.S. Constitution protects the right of law-abiding citizens to keep and bear arms. It does not

give you the right to apply for a permit any more than the 1st Amendment makes you get a permit before you speak. In this case, your driver's license and being 18 gives you the permit required to carry a weapon in Texas. Criminals that have lost this right will have an endorsement removed from their license.

3. **SCHOOL CHOICE:** The money follows the kids and parents who choose charter, private, religious or home school will receive vouchers for a percentage of what the state spends on public schools. By not granting the total amount it means more money per student for public schools and smaller class sizes. By converting to vouchers at the end of each semester this means private schools will not receive a penny until services are provided.

4. **TERM LIMITS:** No office in Texas may be held for more than 8 years. A popular public servant might still try to make a career but they won't be able to hold the same office for

30+ years. One tactic for getting this passed now with current elected officials is to grandfather in those already holding office. They might be able to stay in office for 60 years but their grandchildren will only be able to serve 8 years in any one office.

5. **END TEXAS PROPERTY TAX:** Go big or go home and this is a big one. Replace the property tax with a sales tax will allow people to own the land they buy. Right now, all land is, in effect, rented. Don't believe me? See how long you can go without paying those taxes before the state evicts you and finds another tenant. Replacing these revenues with sales tax is the way to go as everyone will pay a fair share based on what they spend. Exempting food and necessities makes sure the tax does not fall on the poor. This plan also captures tax revenue from visitors, criminals and illegals that might otherwise pay little to no tax.

6. **OUTLAW TEXAS CONVENIENCE ABORTIONS:** The very first part of the

U.S. Constitution says it is meant to protect the "blessings of liberty to ourselves and our posterity." What is posterity but generations yet unborn, including the next one? We know that among those blessings granted to us are life as stated in the Declaration of Independence. The Supreme Court got it wrong chasing shadows in Roe vs. Wade, let us give the current court a chance to fix it.

7. **PUBLIC MEETINGS AND VOTES:** Always open to the public, recorded and available at any time. The state of Texas has no state secrets. Outside of the senate meeting in executive session, all meetings pertaining to public business should be open to the public from any computer screen.

8. **EMINENT DOMAIN:** This must be approved by 12 citizens selected as if it were jury duty. If these 12 people do not approve then the Eminent domain request is denied. The owners of the land and the government will get equal time to make their case and it can only be tried once. This is not a perfect

solution but it is far better than what we have now.

9. **COMPUTER-GENERATED REDISTRICTING PLAN:** Institute a plan starting with the top left voting precinct in Texas, we will add precincts in an attempt to form a square until the population requirement is met. At which time we will start the next district. In this way districts will not be divided to favor either party. This will save time, money and remove the flurry of lawsuits we experience every ten years.

10. **VOTER INTEGRITY:** The strictest one person, one vote election process with fingerprint I.D. for validating ballots. If we get this right, other states will demand it. We must all feel our votes count and that our election process is not corrupt. Penalties for violating the election process must be strengthened. What good are laws if nothing happens even when you are caught breaking them?

I know we said a five-point agenda so between now and 2022 we need to decide which of these ten points become our top five. The others could happen but a clear and consistent message is what we are after and a laundry list does us no good.

We're asking a lot from people and we're also asking them to trust us. How many times have we all been disgusted and disappointed? We can turn those emotions into action by working together.

- We are in need of volunteers in every county.
- We will need candidates to run for office.
- We will ask for candidate donations.
- We will need voters to turn out.

The message is this, to the politicians who sided with Abbott, and to Governor Abbott, "you need to be replaced." These politicians can no longer be protected because they failed to preserve our rights. They called people nonessential and put over three million Texans out of work. At that point those legislatures became nonessential. It is time we return the favor and find their replacements.

We may not have big money behind us but we will have piles of small money. Remember, Texans can take care of our own and we can lead the way in preserving liberty. Once this plan is put into action and it works other states will copy it.

I want you to understand the local and state governments have much more of an impact on our lives than the federal government. If the right people are elected at the state and local level the feds will have even less say than they do now.

The Five Star Agenda Summary

- ✓ How Primary Elections work and who can vote in them.
- ✓ The Five Star Legislative Agenda.
- ✓ We're asking people to work together to preserve liberty.
- ✓ Replacing Governor Abbott and every politician who sided with him.

3

Who Do I Recruit?

Your very first assignment is to find five people that can agree with at least five points of the Five Star Legislative Agenda. This shouldn't be difficult since most people are familiar with these ideas and the issues we face in our state.

Those same five people need to be willing to also find five recruits. This effort will trickle when five more people repeat the process and so on. Feel free to seek more but if you can reach those five then you are a Texas Five Star. You might be wondering, "Where do I find these five people?"

These people are going to be those who are mad at the mandates, had their income affected, their business shut down, or just feel betrayed by their Governor, State Senator or Representative. These people will be the first ones you should talk with and convince to help clean up Texas.

These people can be found at your church, at bars and restaurants or perhaps at neighborhood gatherings. You should find these people within a week or so of deciding to follow TFSP. The power of your help comes when they find five and those people find five and so on because momentum builds unity.

Not everyone will reach this goal, some will get distracted and others will forget all about it. For the patriots who are serious about protecting our liberty they will rise to the task quickly. In theory this process goes from finding the first 100 to finding 500, then 2,500, to 12,500, 62,500, 312,500, and then eventually, the 3.5 million we need for the primary elections. Remember the goal is to reach across Texas and if we work together, we can accomplish this.

Finding more is even better but with this kind of growth just assume the goal of reaching five. Many of us will do much better, my wife and I plan on a hundred or more and we've already begun.

Approaching registered voters and people already voting in the Republican Primaries is a good start. These people will also be more willing to go and find their five as they are currently involved. These people already have a routine for voting in primary elections and only need to be asked to vote a certain way.

Your goal will be to convince them to adopt and use The Five Star Plan for their group. That might be hard and if they're not up for it save yourself some time and drop the subject. We are not asking you to lose friends or family over this. There will always be someone else happy to help and sometimes social media outlets can be a good avenue to find likeminded individuals. Reading Texas news threads and sharing links to the website is a great way to lead others in the right direction. When you are streaming through social media, post about the plan or send a private message to people that share items related to cleaning up Austin or Texas politics in general.

There's also plenty of folks standing in the grocery line and people providing you services. It's easy enough to hand them a business card, a flyer or a brochure if you're in a hurry. Even wearing a t-shirt that says "Ask me about getting rid of Abbott" might recruit more people than you would expect.

Some of you might want to block walk, make phone calls or go to events like a fair or concert. Perhaps asking permission to put up flyers at bars, coffee shops and small businesses would be more to your liking? The flyers are available on our website for free and you can take them to a printer and make as many as you like.

The idea is to get at least five recruits but if you can get a 1,000 why not? We also have a printable monthly calendar, this book, hats and t-shirts available. We encourage you to get at least 5 at some point but you decide which would be best. If all this seems overwhelming don't worry, there is more and we promise to walk you through each step. By doing just a few things each month we can make a huge difference but you need to start now. The deadline to file for the Republican Primary in Texas is December of 2021.

We are asking you to find and recruit people and this might be the hardest thing we ask. These five people need to be willing to step up and be active, they should also consider running for office. Some offices are easy, one example is Republican Precinct Chair. This is a non-paid elected position and they do things like get out the vote or help run elections. They meet as a group four times a year with their County Chair. In these meetings they decide issues concerning the party within that county. If you have never held an elected position this just might be the easiest way to change that.

Why is this such an easy position to gain? About half the precincts across Texas do not have anyone elected and many seats are currently empty. You can get a list of open precinct chairs from your County Clerk or by contacting your County Republican Chair. Most County Chairs will be pleased to help people fill out the appropriate paperwork and since they'll probably be the only person signing up, they will win. Between elections you could just show up to volunteer and they will thank you for filling the position.

Even if the position is currently filled, many chairs never fill out the paperwork to run again and get "appointed" into the position after the election because they have been the precinct chair for years. In the event you fill out the election paperwork and they do not, you win the seat. In the event you both fill out the paperwork then you will have to campaign some, but almost no one will know who either of you are or what function you perform. Expect a 50/50 chance of winning. If you are a Texas Five Star then we will back you and your name will appear on the voters lists for your area. Just let us know and we will be happy to add you to the list.

County Chairs are also unpaid positions and you have to spend a lot more time performing this function. This job is for someone that really wants to be involved and has some time to devote to it.

State Offices and there are many, beginning with Governor. Texas State wide positions have little power granted; they're expensive and difficult to win. The best effort will be focused on voting out the ones who failed to uphold their oath in favor of the primary challengers.

Texas State Representative must be a U.S. citizen, 21 years of age, lived in Texas for 2 years and have lived in the district for at least one year.

Texas State Senator must be a U.S. citizen, 26 years of age, have lived in Texas for five years and inside the district for one year.

These State Representative and State Senator races are where we need to find people to run. The job only pays $600 a month and a couple hundred a day in per diem while in session. This is closer to a volunteer position than an employee. On the other hand, the general session only lasts for 140 days every other year. While in session they receive a couple hundred dollars a day to help pay for hotels and meals and that additional money is tax free. The rest of the year you work your normal job.

Many companies will welcome and allow elected legislators to take time off without being penalized. If you are not sure how your boss would feel about it ask, most times they will be thrilled and might even offer some help in your campaign. It's actually a nice perk to have an elected employee.

The need for recruiting is real and we know there are patriots ready to work together with likeminded individuals. I have no doubt that you can lead in your county or at the state level and find the five we need to succeed.

Who Do I Recruit Summary?

✓ Finding five recruits and growing from there.

✓ Where you can find recruits.

✓ Simple way to market to find recruits.

✓ Basic elected positions recruits can run for.

4

The First Five Steps

You are interested in changing things, so your reason is probably pretty good all on its own. Why are you interested? It might be that you're tired of seeing "Your Guy" go to Austin and not do what they promised and not even try. It may be that you're tired of seeing Republicans control things for 20 years without doing anything that would make you believe they have ever been in charge.

You may be a Democrat that is sick of your party not standing up to the machine but instead being a part of it. Whatever your reason, that is the best reason for you. If someone shows interest ask them, "why they are interested?" let them tell you why. Whatever that person says, that is the best reason for them and try not to debate. Take the win, digest the information and spend time recruiting the next person to the plan.

The best recruits are ones looking for exactly what we're offering, a chance to get rid of the establishment and replace them with real people. However, if they are willing to help because you remind them of a sibling then welcome them to The Five Star Plan.

THE FIRST FIVE STEPS

1. Go to thefivestarplan.com and sign up to receive our newsletter and stay informed. This is our best source of communication as social media is completely unreliable. If for whatever reason you decide TFSP is not for you then unsubscribe at any time. We can't force you to be a part of this and we're far too busy to try and change your mind.

2. Contact by phone or in person five people who you think would be interested in TFSP and ask them if they want to be involved. If they say yes then have them subscribe on the spot, in person or while you have them on the phone. Everyone will receive a welcome email but they may need to be reminded to check their spam folder if it doesn't appear in their inbox. People are busy and life happens but if they sign up immediately it's one less thing you have to ask them to do later.

3. Make a note to check back with them in a few days to see how they're doing in getting their first five or more people on board. Don't feel bad if a few lose interest, it happens, just find another. Never be in the position where you have to push and pull people to be active.

4. Select 5 items from the website resources, or more. This can include TFSP book, free flyers to pass out or items from the shop. The shop is for marketing purposes; you can select what to pass out or display. The reason we let you decide is that you know your situation better

than we do. How great would it be to have people in office with that attitude? If you live or own a business where a yard sign would be the best way to reach out then do that. If you have an outgoing spirit perhaps a t-shirt would make more sense. We leave that up to you and ask you do the same with your recruits.

5. Open your newsletter each week and check back to download the monthly calendar and use it. This calendar includes voting details for getting registered in Primary and General Elections. It will have people that call themselves, "Texas Five Star Candidates." Remember we need candidates or step up yourself. If you meet the requirements then you are qualified and a good heart is far less common but much more valuable, than a Bachelor's of Political Science Degree.

Reaching out to people can be tricky because now days we're dealing with more than just facts, emotion is involved. For the people who like Abbott, what do you even say to them? If you want to get technical read our arguments, they're easy to understand and very simply stated.

The goal isn't to be argumentative with people, remember we're educating. Begin by letting them know what a constitution is and why we have it.

AN EXAMPLE I USE OFTEN

- Tell them it would be like hiring armed guards to protect your house.
- Those guards want you to promise them the job will last at least two years.
- You want to make sure they protect you instead of harming you.
- The agreement you come to is that they must follow certain rules and if they break them, they're fired.

Think about the rules you would make for this home security team. Maybe this list would include, they're not allowed to enter any bedroom unless it's a life and death situation.

No theft would be on the list along with a few others I am sure. Remember you can only fire them if they break the rules. These rules would be written down so there was no misunderstanding and there would be ways to change or add rules as new situations arise.

What you would have is a contract and it would look a lot like a constitution. Those armed guards are our public servants and that home is our town, county, state and nation.

Now when you think about these rules, how many of them would a guard have to break in order to be fired?

Would the other guards be required to make sure your fired guard was removed from the premises and not allowed back into the house?

The government was set up to protect our rights and the constitution is the contract. Governor Abbott broke several of those rules and for the most part our state legislators allowed it. They failed to speak out against his mandates and thus also broke the rules. It is really that simple.

For the people who think an emergency makes it "OKAY" ask them if they have any limits at all on the government. Would you let guards do anything they like to your family or property as long as they yelled "emergency" before breaking the rules that could get them fired?

Here is the oath of office Governor Abbott took when he agreed to be our public SERVANT.

"I, Greg Abbott, do solemnly swear, that I will faithfully execute the duties of the office of governor of the state of Texas, and will to the best of my ability to preserve, protect, and defend the Constitution and the laws of the United States and of this state, so help me GOD."

Notice he swore to protect these things in a certain order. The U.S. Constitution comes first, if there is a conflict between that and the state constitution, the first wins. The Texas Constitution comes next and if there is a conflict between the laws and the Texas Constitution then the Texas Constitution wins. He swore this oath, not just to us but to GOD.

This part comes from the Texas Bill of Rights:

Sec. 6. FREEDOM OF WORSHIP. All men have a natural and indefeasible right to worship Almighty God according to the dictates of their own consciences. No man shall be compelled to attend, erect or support any place of worship, or to maintain any ministry against his consent. No human authority ought, in any case whatever, to control or interfere with the rights of conscience in matters of religion, and no preference shall ever be given by law to any religious society or mode of worship. But it shall be the duty of the Legislature to pass such laws as may be necessary to protect equally every religious denomination in the peaceable enjoyment of its own mode of public worship.

Did Abbott order the churches closed? While we are at it read that last line again and ask yourself, did your state representative and state senator do their duty and defend that right? If not, they have broken their oath and should never be entrusted to guard them again, at any level.

The highlight of this piece is the following section. "No human authority ought, in any case whatever, to control or interfere with the rights of conscience in matters of religion…"

Sec. 9. SEARCHES AND SEIZURES. The people shall be secure in their persons, houses, papers and possessions, from all unreasonable seizures or searches, and no warrant to search any place, or to seize any person or thing, shall issue without describing them as near as may be, nor without probable cause, supported by oath or affirmation.

Did Abbott order private businesses to close? When the state closes a business for a day it is a "taking." That is private property and property you are not allowed to use is not property you own. If the state ordered you to only drive every other day, they would be taking half of your car. If I move into your house, I am taking your house, even if I say it is only for a couple of weeks to "flatten the curve" it is still theft. Was there a warrant when Abbott shut down those businesses?

Sec. 16. BILLS OF ATTAINDER; EX POST FACTO OR RETROACTIVE LAWS; IMPAIRING OBLIGATION OF CONTRACTS. No bill of attainder, ex post facto law, retroactive law, or any law impairing the obligation of contracts, shall be made.

Did Abbott order gyms to shut down? Some people had contracts with these gyms. Some even paid for their yearly membership up front. This clearly impaired the obligation of those contracts.

Sec. 17. TAKING PROPERTY FOR PUBLIC USE; SPECIAL PRIVILEGES AND IMMUNITIES; CONTROL OF PRIVILEGES AND FRANCHISES.

(a) No person's property shall be taken, damaged, or destroyed for or applied to public use without adequate compensation being made, unless by the consent of such person, and only if the taking, damage, or destruction is for:(1) the ownership, use, and enjoyment of the property, notwithstanding an incidental use, by: (A) the State, a political subdivision of the State, or the public at large; or (B) an entity granted the power of eminent domain under law; or (2) the elimination of urban blight on a particular parcel of property.(b) In this section, "public use" does not include the taking of property under Subsection (a) of this section for transfer to a private entity for the primary purpose of economic development or enhancement of tax revenues.(c) On or after January 1, 2010, the legislature may enact a general, local, or special law granting the power of eminent domain to an entity only on a two-thirds vote of all the members elected to each house. (d) When a person's property is taken under Subsection (a) of this section, except for the use of the State, compensation as described by Subsection (a) shall be first made, or secured by a deposit of money; and no irrevocable or uncontrollable grant of special privileges or immunities shall be made; but all privileges and franchises granted by the Legislature, or created under its authority, shall be subject to the control thereof.

Did Abbott order private businesses to close? Not only was this a taking but under this law there is no authority in the state constitution to allow it. Even if there were such an authority, the very FIRST thing that would have to be done would be to compensate or pay the people impacted in advance, was this done?

Sec. 19. DEPRIVATION OF LIFE, LIBERTY, PROPERTY, ETC. BY DUE COURSE OF LAW. No citizen of this State shall be deprived of life, liberty, property, privileges or immunities, or in any manner disfranchised, except by the due course of the law of the land.

Did Abbott hand authority to County Judges in Texas to hand out "Stay at Home" mandates? They called these "Quarantines" but look up the word in the dictionary.

QUARANTINE DEFINITION: "a state, period, or place of isolation in which people or animals that have arrived from elsewhere or been exposed to infectious or contagious disease are placed."

Now I ask you, did the residents in El Paso County, Texas "arrive here from somewhere else" or are they residents of El Paso County, Texas? Did the Judge offer or even attempt to prove that every single resident had been exposed to an infectious or contagious disease?

So, if the thing they are calling a "quarantine" does not match the definition of that word what does it match? Try "House Arrest, the state of being kept as a prisoner in one's own house, rather than in a prison." Was there a trial? Was there even a charge? But there was a sentence.

Sec. 33. PUBLIC ACCESS TO AND USE OF PUBLIC BEACHES. (a) In this section, "public beach" means a state-owned beach bordering on the seaward shore of the Gulf of Mexico, extending from mean low tide to the landward boundary of state-owned submerged land, and any larger area extending from the line of mean low tide to the line of vegetation bordering on the Gulf of Mexico to which the public has acquired a right of use or easement to or over the area by prescription or dedication or has established and retained a right by virtue of continuous right in the public under Texas common law.

(b) The public, individually and collectively, has an unrestricted right to use and a right of ingress to and egress from a public beach. The right granted by this subsection is dedicated as a permanent easement in favor of the public.

(c) The legislature may enact laws to protect the right of the public to access and use a public beach and to protect the public beach easement from interference and encroachments.

(d) This section does not create a private right of enforcement.

Did Abbott close the public beaches? No matter how briefly, he violated the Texas State Constitution. Have you even kept track of how many violations up to this point? Me either, because even one is too many.

Understand this, these violations would be true even if the legislature had "approved" all of these measures. Don't believe it? Look at this:

Sec. 29. BILL OF RIGHTS EXCEPTED FROM POWERS OF GOVERNMENT AND INVIOLATE.

To guard against transgressions of the high powers herein delegated, we declare that everything in this "Bill of Rights" is excepted out of the general powers of government, and shall forever remain inviolate, and all laws contrary thereto, or to the following provisions, shall be void.

So, the Texas government, every aspect of it, does not have the power to do what Governor Greg Abbott has mandated or what some County Judges have mandated. There's more.

ARTICLE 2, SECTION 1. The powers of the government of the State of Texas shall be divided into three distinct departments, each of which shall be confided to a separate body of magistracy; to wit: Those which are legislative to one, those which are executive to another, and those which are judicial to another; and no person, or collection of persons, being of one of these departments, shall exercise any power properly attached to either of the others, except in the instances herein expressly permitted.

The State House and Senate gave the Governor powers to act in their place during an emergency. They can no more grant the Governor power through law than they can take away his powers through law, it would require a change to the Texas Constitution. The entire Emergency Powers Act is unconstitutional according to Article II, Section 1 of the Texas State Constitution.

If the Governor does not have this authority and the legislature does not have this authority then how can they possibly hand this power over to the County Judges? As I said, any Judge that used this power, any Sheriff that enforced this power and any State Legislator that stood by and let this happen has broken their oath and betrayed your trust.

Now can you see why regular people need to step forward? How can we possibly complain about the federal government or other states when we will not hold our own state officials, from both parties, accountable?

The First Five Steps Summary

- ✓ The personalities you are seeking to recruit.

- ✓ The five steps to follow and repeat.

- ✓ How to explain the importance of the constitution.

- ✓ The violation breakdown of the Texas Constitution.

5

Can We Really Do This?

As I write this, it's the 244th birthday of the U.S. Marine Corps and tomorrow will be Veterans' Day. The only reason I mention this or care is that my son is a Marine and my daughter served in the Army. My father fought in WWII and my grandfather fought in WWI. I have brothers who served during the Korean and Vietnam Wars and myself and little brother served during Desert Storm.

When you thank most veterans for serving, they will tell you they did not see combat. Thank a combat veteran and they will tell you they were never wounded. Thank a veteran with scars and they will tell you they were not disabled. Thank a disabled vet and they will tell you about the ones that did not make it back alive.

I am positive if you could thank a fallen hero, they would tell you they were just doing their job and to thank someone that made a difference.

Generations have fought and died to give us the freedoms we have, or had until recently. There is no excuse not to take the time and protect these freedoms for the next generation and the ones after that. People that we never knew and who never knew us gave everything. The Five Star Plan isn't asking for anything near that level of sacrifice.

It is November 2020 as I write this; there are groups of people on the right and left who are itching for a civil war. As a student of history, a veteran and a person that has seen what conflict looks like, I can tell you that what many of these people want, is a fantasy. A quick, easy fix and I understand their frustration. The last Civil War and

GOD willing, the only one, cost more American lives than every other war we have ever fought, combined.

When people tell me that our political division has never been greater, I respond with, "May, 1861-650,000 dead Americans." Yeah, it's been worse.

What are we asking again? Just to get five new people to vote in the Republican Primary of 2022. Make sure those five recruits are registered and if they're not registered to vote then lead them in that direction. Make sure they have the Five Star list of candidates and make sure they actually go vote in the 2022 Primary. If you can get more people that is great but just five is what we are asking and of course ask them to do the same.

We have a target of 5 million voters. Half a million might be enough but with five million it will be a landslide in favor of the voters against the political elites. We are not asking for donations or a ton of your time but we are asking for some.

Perhaps after you vote you might even consider standing at a legal distance from the polling place and pass out our list of recommended candidates. Print them off from the website and get copies made the day prior. Maybe get your five new primary voters to join you and maybe the 25 they asked to help and so on. Get Five Star t-shirts to help you stand out and it's possible that on that day, just maybe, we can get people to change their minds. So often all you have to do is just ask.

For too long, a small handful of people have been giving us a "magicians choice" when it came to voting. For those of you that are not familiar with that term let me explain. A magician wants you to pick his right hand. He extends both hands and asks you to pick one. If you point to the right hand, he will say, "very well" and then open his hand to complete the trick. If you were to point to the left hand he would say "very well, you want this one to go away." Then he would open his right hand to complete the trick. In this way you would always "choose" the right hand. You think you have a choice but the choice has been made for you.

By voting in the Primary Election and voting for fellow citizens that have never held office before you are voting for people that have no history of being dishonest in public office. These same people have never once failed you in the capacity of our present legislators. They might eventually fail you, but at least they do not have a history of it.

Don't let people dazzle you with their resume or how many years they have been elected officials. If they had done such a great job then why is it all such a mess? Don't let them demand your vote because of higher education, my thermometer has more degrees and I don't let that run my life.

Too many of us think we should vote for Dr. Evil over Forrest Gump. The Doctor has the intelligence, education and experience but Forrest has a heart and cares more about what is right and wrong. Truth be told many people that never attended so much as a college party score higher on IQ tests than some college graduates and in many cases have read far more books. Get to know the candidates, attend forums, and ask questions.

We currently have some excellent public servants, like any group there are good ones and bad ones. The good ones we will recommend and support, the others we will try to replace.

Can we do this? Of course. We are spending almost two years recruiting voters one-on-one. We are deciding which politicians to keep, and which ones to replace. Our 3.5 million new voters will not be swayed by fake commercials or yard signs. I would love to put people in office that spent almost nothing in the Primary Election so that we can focus our resources in the General Election where the races might be tight.

- Can you get five people to vote for someone better than Abbott in the Primary Election of 2022?
- Can you get more than five people active?

If you answered yes to either question, then yes, we can succeed. Once we have the Primary Election then that just leaves the General Election. In Texas we almost all know who wins in any given race before it even starts. If we get the people to the polls for the Primary, we can contact them again and remind them of the General Election. They will already have some skin in the game and momentum builds unity.

We will show people who haven't bothered in the past what a difference they can make in who serves. When our candidates reach Austin, we can show these same people what a difference they made in what gets done. With those two items of proof in hand it will be far easier to keep people involved and get them back to the polls on a regular basis.

2020 has been perhaps the worst year of my life. The people I have lost, the freedoms I have seen taken and the hatred I have witnessed has been depressing. However, this year has reminded many people why we have limits on what governments can do. This year also reminded us why freedom is so important and exactly how quickly it can disappear if we allow it.

When Rick Perry was governor of Texas, he tried to make a vaccine mandatory for all females below the age of 18. Eventually he had to concede because he didn't have the power to enforce it. Why? Texans said "No." The vaccine might have been a great idea but we were lied to from the start when it was presented as a vaccine against cancer. Later we were told it would be mandatory and we said "No again." Then we were told our children could not attend public schools if they did not get it and we said, "Fine, we will homeschool."

Public schools had no problem enforcing the mandate right up to the time Texas parents told the schools we would pull 20-30% of our kids and they would lose funding. At that point it was the schools on the phone to the governor's office demanding the idea go away, not just us.

At the time, people asked me "why are you not angrier with the proposed requirements?" I informed them that I was raising two kids, working two jobs and was actively engaged in a combination of apathy and revolution, I called it "apolution." I did not care what the governor said and would ignore it and most Texans were of the same mind set. We did not protest; we did not organize but we got what we wanted and Perry was not allowed into the medical decisions of my family.

Why get so involved this time? Because this time I simply cannot ignore the direction Texas is headed. If we would have organized, protested and kicked Governor Perry out of politics, we would not find ourselves in the present situation. Outlawing church services? Picking what business owners get to stay open and which have to close?

I do not have the keys to the church or the keys to these closed businesses and I cannot ignore or let this go away. Any man that broke his oath to GOD so many times, in so many ways, for such a length of time, cannot be allowed to continue or the next tyrant will go even further.

This year has allowed us all to see what happens when "we the people" allow it. Just as we could not have imagined this happening in the United States, let alone Texas, we do not want to admit it could get even worse. It can get worse, if we do nothing.

Can we succeed? Of course, can we afford not to? We are stepping up to honor every person who has ever put their lives on the line or given it to further the ideals of this nation.

I put Martin Luther King in that category as much as any fallen soldier. I put JFK in that group along with the people I knew and placed in small plastic bags while in the military. I am not exaggerating the importance of this in any way.

This plan to clean out the corrupt and self-serving political class is possible because of the terrible events of 2020. It has shown people with no interest or concern with politics that they can be affected. It has unveiled they can even be killed by public servants who have ignored their oaths and the constraints placed on them by the laws they were supposed to uphold.

We can succeed because people that just wanted to be left alone were not left alone. Shelley Luther did not plan on getting into politics. She has kids to raise and a business to run until she was not allowed. She came within a few percentage points of winning a State Senate seat. Her Republican opponent only won by spending three million dollars and openly embracing BLM activists and the Democratic Party to help him block walk. Where will his Democrats be in the primaries next year?

Don't mess with people that want to be left alone, they do not appreciate it. Many people said Abbott took the measures he did in order to "get our attention." Trust me, the last thing anyone in Austin should ever want is our complete and undivided attention.

Can We Do This Summary

- ✓ The oath people have taken to protect our freedoms.
- ✓ A Civil War is not the solution to preserving liberty.
- ✓ Why we should have stopped Perry.
- ✓ Answering how we can do this.

6

The Candidate

Do you want to be a candidate but not quite sure you are the right person for the job? Great, remember that most people in the bible never thought they were qualified when God called them to lead. Most people are humble, more than they realize. You need to think about running, talk it over with your family and pray. If your 51% sure then go for it.

Whatever office you plan on running for the first step is to look up the qualifications. Don't worry about what to look for in a candidate so much, find out what is actually required to run for that position.

To be a Congress person you would have to live in the state you are running, be a US citizen for the past seven years and be at least 25 year of age. That's it according to the U.S. Constitution.

Additional offices have other requirements. If you go to the Texas Secretary of State website, the qualifications are clearly stated for each elected position. Once you know you are qualified, we can move to the next thing.

Now ask yourself the following questions. This might take a little research but it's necessary before proceeding forward.

1. Does the person holding that office right now follow their oath and the constitution?
2. Do they side with the voters over the governor?
3. Have they pushed legislation even if it was not popular with their colleagues in Austin of which you approve?

If the elected legislator has approval on all three then you might want to run for a different office. If they don't meet approval then carry on because now you have the first campaign issues for running against them in the Primary Election.

The next area of importance is establishing a campaign theme. A theme that includes five stars and clearly states the following:

1. You intend to follow the Texas Constitution.
2. You intend to keep your oath of office.
3. You intend to oppose anyone that does not.

These three points would have seemed laughable not long ago but now this sets you apart. This theme would make you a public servant instead of an elected master and tracks with every candidate The Five Star Plan is supporting.

When people hear one of our candidates speak, they hear all of our candidates speak. This shows voters you are part of a state-wide movement and will encourage them to support your run.

If you're not a public speaker, that is fine. Speaking in front of an audience has been found to be the scariest thing in the world; it out ranks death. I would like to see where dying in front of an audience ranks the next time, they take that survey.

There is an organization called Toastmasters and I strongly urge anyone running for county or offices above to join, even if only for a few weeks. Short of that you can practice giving a speech in front of a mirror or for your family until you have a handle on it. The more you practice, the easier it gets.

If you video and play back a speech for the first time you might want to crawl under a table because there will be things about yourself you never realized. I had the honor of hearing Ed Means speak before his death and he was a great speaker but he could not stop touching his face and it was distracting. I try to have a plan for my hands to either grip a microphone or podium so they do not distract. When I am passionate about a topic my arms tend to move, I try to make sure they don't distract from the message by keeping them low or to the side. When you concentrate on giving the audience the information, you'll be more focused and less worried about what it looks like.

How do you get people to vote for you? We are doing an awful lot of the work to get you elected. The person that asked you to run, the people that said it was a great idea, these are called supporters and I would suggest you turn them into volunteers immediately.

Now, back to the voters. Are you a member of a church, civic group or club? Where do you work and do you come into contact with a lot of people each day? None of these things are required but it gives you an idea of how many people around you might be willing to support what you're doing. Everyone at my work knows I'm involved in politics and I'm the first person they go to when they have a question about government or politics.

With all of these people, you need to ask them or some of them to volunteer for you. The best approach is to inquire if they would ever help out "in the future" or if you should "decide to run." A hypothetical normally gets the best response and once they have said yes, immediately get their contact information. If you have someone that has agreed to help run your campaign, that information goes straight to the person who will reach out and remind them they agreed to help.

I promised we would get to voters and here we are. Where you live makes a huge difference in how you campaign. If you live in the suburbs, I envy you. It is perhaps the best area for people to knock doors.

If you live in a city then campaign anywhere a crowd would gather. Places like bus stops, open business courtyards and restaurants are all good options. Entering places like apartment buildings may be difficult as the majority are gated communities. Being at the front entrance at the end of the day handing out flyers might be a better way to go.

In rural areas the houses are spread out and many of them have gates away from the home. It is hard to call first as many people have cell phones and getting the number before you arrive is difficult. In person is still the best way to meet people to get them involved. Once you have an organization get those people to research contacts and set up a route. This will save a lot of time and time is one thing you will never have enough of. Good planning helps you use the time you have available in the best way possible.

With the bar mandates those businesses have lost a lot and they might let you have a few minutes to speak on stage. They may even allow you to pass a hat to help get you elected. Also ask if you could post or pass out campaign flyers while you are there.

At this point you have a candidate or you are the candidate. This is awesome, because we might need more than one and you have already proven you can convince someone to run for office, even if it is just yourself.

Believe me when I say, "You will have doubts from time to time." If you, or the person you recruited are not the ideal candidate ask yourself, "Is it better than what we have?" If the answer is yes then you found the best person for the job. Quite frankly I am to the point where a lottery system might be better than how we do things now. Choosing a group of random citizens, I am convinced they would do a better job than the group we have in office right now.

The Candidate Summary

✓ Selecting an office, you want to run.

✓ Researching the competition, who you plan to run against.

✓ Agreeing to TFSP campaign theme.

✓ How to prepare and find supporters.

7

The Office

There will be an abundance of target offices we need to run for in the 2022 Primaries. I'm going to begin with important local offices because those are the ones that impact our lives more than those who sit in D.C. or the state capital.

Political parties are known for building county organizations because those boundaries are fixed. Counties do not change like district and precinct lines change every 10 years. Within those county lines you have Precinct Chairs and each precinct has a chair position. Across the state only about half of these offices are filled and this seat is an unpaid elected position.

Precinct Chairs meet at least four times a year and decide things pertaining to the party at a county level. If you don't have a lot of time but want to assist with elections and help get out the vote this might be the office for you. The great thing about this position is that if you are new and not sure about serving in an elected office you only have to fill out the paperwork to get elected in most cases. Half of the time there will never be an opponent. Even the people currently serving often skip filling out the paperwork. If you are the only one to register you win without even being on the ballot.

If you do have an opponent most people have no idea who either of you are or what your office does. It will be a coin flip unless you do a lot of campaigning and most people do not spend any money to seek this office. For an in-depth look at this office go to the Texas Republican Party website.

County Chair would be the next step up in the party. This position is also unpaid but carries more responsibility. You would be running the four yearly meetings, filing paperwork and are often the single most important person in the county making sure the party wins elections. This seat takes more time but still is not anywhere near a full-time position unless you choose to make it such. The handbook is available on the Texas Republican Party website.

Texas County Commissioners run the county and care for county roads. Some are more active than others but as a rule it is a full-time job that pays a living wage. It does not sound like an exciting political position but imagine if these Commissioners decided a County Judge could get paid a dollar a year if they utilize Emergency Executive Powers the governor granted them? Part of running a county is deciding salaries.

County Judge heads up the Commissioners Court. They preside over the Commissioner's Court and they're closer to mini governors than judges in

Texas. A law degree is not required, or any degree to qualify. You just need to get elected.

Like commissioners it usually pays a living wage and should be a full-time job in most counties. If your County Judge issued mandates and enforced shut downs when "given" the power by Governor Abbott then they must be replaced. Even if they share your last name they need to be voted out. There is no place in our political system for anyone that would trample your rights and break their oath of office.

County Sheriff is perhaps the most vital office in the county for preserving liberty. Most people associate law enforcement with incarceration and enforcing law on citizens but that is not their actual oath of office. As the supreme law enforcement authority in a county they can refuse to enforce unconstitutional laws put out by anyone in the Oval Office, Austin or the County Judge. This power has been upheld for them in the Supreme Court and if your sheriff enforced Abbott's unconstitutional mandates then they violated their oath. Good sheriffs protect you from law breakers, both those in government and outside of government. They take an oath to defend the constitution, the laws and are there to defend your rights and protect you. If your sheriff does not see it that way then you need a new sheriff.

Ask candidates if they are members or are planning on joining the Constitutional Sheriff and Police Officer Associations. Ask them if they would enforce state or federal laws that violate the plain language of the U.S. and State Constitutions. If the answer is anything like "The law is the law." They need to be educated or replaced. They are the actual armed guards we hired to protect our families and our property and they need to know they work for us and not the other way around.

Judges that are elected to office are in a tough position. To campaign for an office, we are familiar with people telling us how they will act and what they will do once in office. Judges cannot do that. If they tell you how they will rule on a hypothetical case without even hearing the case then they are not Judges at all but politicians in the worst sense of the word. They are vital but cannot speak, we need to pick the best people, but we are the ones forced to do the research or rely on recommendations.

Most of us were taught not to vote straight party but to vote for the people. We were told not to vote for people or issues we know nothing about but to skip that race and allow more informed voters to make the call. This would be ideal but if your party is in power across the board but has very few elected judges then the other side is not following that advice.

Research the judges but failing that, just vote for the ones in your political party. Very often that is the only thing you have to go by on election day. If you think this means party over people you are wrong. This book is meant to toss out politicians of both stripes if they are not protecting your rights. Judges are important in protecting those rights so if all else is equal, vote for judges in your party.

Texas Attorney General is the chief legal officer of the state. As of this writing Ken Paxton is under investigation by the FBI. He has delayed his trial on securities violations for five years in a separate legal case. He has changed out his legal staff that reported what they saw as corruption in his behavior during 2020. Let us add he's steadfastly not commented on any mandate, law change or proposed mandates as they pertain to the Texas Constitution including Abbott changing election law which both the U.S. and Texas Constitution forbids.

For people that paid attention, when the Houston Democratic Mayor decided to cancel the Republican State Convention in a Presidential election year, but allowed 60,000 protesters into his city, Ken Paxton sided with this Democrat in his official capacity. Convince me these things happened because the sitting governor of Texas did not wish to be seen on stage while his own party greeted him with a boo and a modified salute.

Lieutenant Governor, this is actually the most powerful position in Texas. The governor is the manager but the lt. governor is president of the state senate and sits on many legislative boards including the one that decides the state budget. Once things are decided in the senate and the house the governor can veto or sign, but it will not get to his desk if the lt. governor does not want it there.

As with so many of our elected officials our current Lieutenant Governor, Dan Patrick started out with a bang. He was endorsed into office by Tea Party Patriots and among strong conservatives he was a lion. The following election we began to see him distance himself from almost daily meetings with these people and by his third term he would not take their calls and is now the problem, not the cure. Grandstanding aside he sided with Democrats and the Governor rather than the state constitution, his oath or the people of Texas.

Governor, under the constitution of Texas is a pretty weak office. Remember Texas had just fought a dictator when they first wrote the state constitution and wanted no part of tyranny. The role of a Texas Governor is very clear.

In 2020 Abbott ignored that altogether, one would have to ask him what his limits were that year. The following are the actual legal powers of the governor's office.

- He is the head of the military.
- He can call legislators into a special session.
- He can make suggestions about spending.
- He can inform the state about budget needs.
- He can deal with other states and the federal government.
- He can pardon and parole.

There are a number of people that could run against Abbott in the 2022 primaries. It is my hope the best candidates will not cancel each other out at the polls. This election will decide if the Texas governor will ever be bound by the constitution again. These men or women need to decide if beating Abbott is more important than which person wins.

We have 150 State Representatives and 31 Senators, with perhaps 5 being worthy of holding office. We need to find candidates for most of these. If you find yourself seeking to run against a great representative or senator, then don't. There are other offices you can be running for that need you more.

I've listed the positions we need to find people for in the next election and the one after that, and the one after that. Sorry that this isn't a quick fix and a high five but as Thomas Jefferson said and we so quickly forgot,

"The price of liberty is eternal vigilance."

The Office Summary

✓ Covering unpaid county elected offices.

✓ Covering paid county elected offices.

✓ Covering elected Judges offices.

✓ Covering state level offices.

8

Make It Happen

What would it be like to have people in office for only a couple of terms and then go home? We would have to look at the first hundred years of this country to find out. Men served for a slap on the back if they did well or actual tar and feathers if they had done wrong.

Being in office and famous did not mean you would be re-elected, which is why Davy Crockett died at the Alamo instead of serving in the U.S. Congress.

If you recall, the founders were mainly in their late 20's when the country fought for our freedom in the Revolutionary War. Their powdered wigs make us think they were old men but most older men don't go toe to toe with a superpower.

How would things be if you went to Austin or Congress for just two or three terms? If you were not devoted to re-election for life, if you were not always in an election year or one leading up to an election year, which is all of them?

Most of us would do our best and head home, proud of the yes and no votes we cast for our community and our family. Imagine no long-range career advancement calculations to cloud our judgement. No chance to get used to the "but that is how we've always done it" attitude that causes so many to start out as heroes and end up cogs.

I recently spoke to a chair person about a career politician and asked, "How did they ever allow him into any office?" She said, that he had replaced a really corrupt individual and that he had been a super hero in his first term. She continued saying, something happened to him and she didn't even recognize him anymore. She then cheered up and said, "He's your problem now."

The Five Star Plan is not a new party nor is it a group. It is a plan that I hope the Republican Party and other conservative and patriot groups will adopt. The goal is to return the Republican party to what it should be, a political party for conservatives. To make this happen, the first goal is to recruit those five people.

Every day you speak to people when going about your business. If the topic of politics surfaces, you will often hear, "What can I do?" Many people have given up on having an impact. Some have allowed others to convince them that others need to do great things to have an impact.

Many times, our educational system has led them to believe that public servants are above them in power and that is not the case. Public officials have many constraints placed on them that you and I don't have on our lives. When you get this question, "What can I do?" remind them that they are above their servants and follow up by offering examples and explaining things in a non-complex way. A great place to begin is to remind them, "We're the public, they're the servant."

Tell them they can run for office or help someone else run for office. Ask them if they approve of the way the country is headed. If they don't approve, then ask them if they are willing to spend an hour a week to make it better. With this approach, a lot of people will answer "no" but there will be times when you will get a "yes." Perhaps the next time you ask you will hear a "yes" from someone who rejected you in the past.

Face to face is always the best way to recruit but if you want to pass out flyers, business cards, wear a shirt or place an ad then go right ahead. The voter is not as constrained as politicians or political parties and that makes you, person for person, much more effective.

When my wife and I started a Tea Party during the Obama administration, we had no idea how to invite people. We started a website, printed up some t-shirts and found a coffee shop willing to host our meetings. We started with a few people and went door-to-door as a group asking people to join us at our next event. Recruiting was ongoing, something we did every other month and the monthly meetings involved ideas on how to make an impact and discussing current events. We also helped other counties recruit members to their group or attended peaceful protests.

Once you have volunteers you are better off having something for them to do and there should always be something to do. You might have a local need and your group can help by gathering signatures. Many people are willing to help if you're only asking for a signature. While they're gathering that information, you can ask them about joining a group to help out in the future.

Another idea would be to schedule a phone bank party. Come up with a script such as a survey and pass off a list of numbers to each invite. You may want to role play prior to phone calling just to make sure everyone is on the same page.

PHONE SCRIPT

"Hello, my name is _____ and I am calling from_____, is this a good time?"

This introduction lets them know who you are, what group you are with and that you know they might be in the middle of something.

If you get a "not a good time" response, ask them when would be a better time and make a note to follow up.

If you get the go ahead ask their opinion on whether they thought there was any fraud in the 2020 election, their response will tell you pretty much which direction they lean.

You can then ask if they have ever thought about getting more involved in politics or running for office. This gives them a chance to tell you why or why not, as people tend to explain themselves with a prompt like instead of a yes or no.

The third question might be, "Would you like to attend the next meeting of the (-------) group in order to share your opinions?"

If they say yes then share the time and date of the next meeting or event. Thank them for their time and be sure to close with saying, "I look forward to meeting you." You might even throw in something like, "I'll be the one in the red shirt." Then make a note of that call.

The day before the meeting call to remind them they agreed to attend and let them know everyone is looking forward to their attendance. Getting new people to group meetings will create a lot of excitement among members because people can see it's growing. Some people will cancel and if they do ask if it would be okay to call back and invite them to the next meeting. Don't get to the point where you are bothering people but some will need a little additional nudge.

If they back out, don't get discouraged. You succeeded in identifying another person that will not waste your time in the future. This makes your next phone attempt more focused. The people that say no are still providing valuable training. When you call the next person, they might be eager to join a group like yours. By the time you have a hundred calls completed you won't even need a script because you've become a pro. Remember, you can't make them agree but you can decide to dial one more number.

MEETINGS

There are groups of people who tend to agree with you. In my case it's Veterans, Republicans, Patriot and Tea Party groups. These organizations normally have monthly meetings and have people attending on a regular basis. If you can get to one of those events and pass out flyers or cards you might gain a few supporters. You might even want to speak at one of these events as a way to find candidates in your county. Most groups are open to hearing from speakers that agree with their views.

Social media is another avenue to share information and perhaps recruit people. Another idea is to comment on social media news feeds.

Replying or messaging can gain a few supporters and sometimes great friends.

Educating people can be exhausting, it sounds like we're acting smarter, but that's not the case. I have met people that agree with me but do not understand many of the issues they're upset with are not just wrong but illegal. Most will be surprised to learn about things they did not know. If you have a better way of explaining, they can use that explanation to spread the word themselves. Another highlight, is when you're in a group setting and you begin to hear the words you spoke, repeated.

If you read the U.S. Constitution, try to find what some people describe as "being there" in the text. For example, separation of church and state has gone from not having mandated religion to mandating the government not spend money to promote, endorse or support religion. There is no justification for infringing the Second Amendment in any way. When this amendment was written it was common to outfit a ship with cannons. These ship owners did not need a permit to buy or install cannons and would have laughed if you suggested they ought to.

I was talking to a judge the other day and commented that you could get through law school without ever seeing the text of the constitution. We teach legal findings, opinions and precedent to such a degree that the simple words of the constitution no longer apply. We have nearly ceased being a constitutional republic and have become a legal precedent republic. To illustrate, what do the words "shall not" mean to you? What does the word "infringe" mean to you? How much education is required to convert "shall not" into "yeah, you can do that."

The other thing you can do is read, "The Federalist Papers." These writings will let you know exactly what the founders thought about what they wrote. The book, "1984" by Orwell will show you why the meaning of words is important and why they seem to be changing. "Fahrenheit 451" will explain why some people are set on getting rid of certain books. "The Law" by Frederick Bastiat is online and shares how law is being used to take instead of being used to defend.

Even basic civic activities, like where and how they register to vote has become mysteries for people, many of whom agree with you on political issues. Educate, be educated and keep learning. Don't become just smart enough to pay taxes, become smart enough to influence how those taxes are spent.

Identify who and what is worth your time, money, energy and vote. Ask questions of that person that wants to be Sheriff. Will they uphold the constitution over the law? Will they enforce mandates from a governor?

That person running for County Judge, will they take the authority gifted to them by the governor or will they stay within the bounds of the constitution? The person running for County Commissioner, will they vote to lower the pay of an out of control County Judge?

Candidates can say whatever they like and act certain ways to get elected. Then they turn around afterwards and do the complete opposite; we have all seen that. Take note and spread the word when that happens.

I would prefer just about anyone to a person that has proven their word and oath is worthless. Even the other party might be better than praising a scoundrel, at least you have a chance of getting a better candidate next time rather than being saddled with a rat for the rest of your life.

ACTION

Action seems pretty common since that word without movement amounts to nothing. Every single one of us can choose to take action. Writing our representative and senators and sending letters to the editor are a few traditional ways to respond. Posting on social media and sending emails have become the modern way to take action. We also act when we vote. We act when we choose to stay near the election site asking people to please vote for a certain candidate or to vote against one.

Finding people that want to vote the same way and getting them registered is a very important action. Calling these people and getting them to go vote in the primary is another. How many people could you get to agree and vote in the next Primary Election if you started today? Five, ten maybe a hundred?

The Primary Election is where all the people get narrowed down to the few who will appear on the General Election ballot. The primaries are more important than most elections in Texas as this is where the seat selection is made.

In the General Election, most of Texas will vote for whatever Republican wins in the primary and most cities will choose whoever wins in the Democratic Primary.

It's quite unfortunate that our General Elections have turned into a team sporting event. After all, we're giving these people the power to protect our freedom and uphold the constitution. Shouldn't we be placing more action and emphasis on our Primary Elections?

MONITOR

The price of freedom is eternal vigilance, you will hear me repeat this phrase often. We have allowed our representatives to stay in office after passing laws and voting for bills, of which we don't approve. We keep rewarding them by continuing to vote and support their reelections just because they have an R or D by their name. At some point we're partly to blame for the corruption that's been occurring for many years.

Pay attention to what these elected officials are doing. Listen to the people that approve of their actions and be attentive to those who disapprove. Look into things by doing your own research and ask those that hold elected office questions from time to time, an email is fine. If they don't reply then pick up the phone or attend a meeting where they may be speaking and put them on the spot in front of voters.

Recruit and find five likeminded individuals and ask them to vote in the Republican Primaries and find five more. That's all I'm really asking you to do; this is the essence of The Five Star Plan. This is a simple process and I will admit at times it may not always be easy.

If you agree with this plan then start now. If you take a month to find five people and they take a month and so on, you will be responsible for 78 thousand people showing up to vote in the 2022 Primary Elections. Just you alone, get the ball rolling today because I bet you can think of at least two people you can contact right now.

Explain to those five what the elected did wrong. This is not difficult but you have to know what rules were broken and why it matters. The following is a factual event, a list of Republicans met with Democrats in late 2020 in a closed-door meeting that not every legislator was allowed to attend. They met and decided who the next Texas Speaker of the House would be in violation of the Republican party rules.

The Texas Constitution says, all meetings of the legislature are public except the Texas Senate while in Executive Session. These elected legislatures conducted public business in secret. What they were promised and agreed to remains a mystery and they did this while not in session, while the capital was closed. They broke their oath and their pledge.

Go online and research, "Dade Phelan's supporters for House Speaker," this will show you the results of that meeting. If your representative was one of the "Republicans" that failed to follow the party rules, then these people have gone past not having loyalty to the people. They have no loyalty to the party, the rules, the constitution or the people. This means they now only have loyalty to each other and their own agendas.

If picking the Speaker of the House in a secret meeting is too technical, what about voting to allow China to operate drones over Texas? Look up the 2018 vote that ended with a defeat of over 50 State Representatives, many were Republican, that voted to do just that. Now look up Texas Bill 4448 and click the highlighted text where you can see who voted to pass this bill. They voted for this bill even after it was pointed out that China has a law requiring a "backdoor" be installed on drones they manufacture so they can be operated by the Chinese government at will. This bill would have allowed China to collect information on military bases, infrastructure and individuals within Texas. No surprise, the two lists contain many of the same names.

"What do we do?" I hear this all the time; it is the reason this book was written. What you do is everything possible. As a legal citizen you vote, especially in the primaries. You have a phone that's always handy and capable of giving you more information than anyone can possibly use. The phone offers simple ways to share your views with millions of people. An elected official often has less freedom than a voter, you are not nearly as constrained by re-election concerns or public opinion. Get the word out so people can see the Texas swamp within both political parties because the corruption is real.

You can ask business owners if they will post your flyers. Organize events, even if they're just monthly at a local coffee shop. This offers an opportunity to encourage, plan and share ideas for finding and meeting new candidates. Put up a website or social media group and make sure to share it with us at TFSP so we can add it to the resources. Business cards from Vistaprint are cheap, get a box for your site or the one you joined and pass them out to store owners and likeminded people.

The short-term goal is to get Abbott censured by the majority of our counties so that he does not run in 2022. His support or endorsement then becomes toxic. By making an example of Abbott through the power of the everyday voter we prevent such overreach from future governors.

Long term we can do the same thing with other elected officials. Republicans that get elected using the platform and refuse to act like Republicans are not conservatives? We can get rid of them in the same manner. Censure is a tool to remove corrupt politicians from the system and it works. That is how we got rid of Strauss and Bonnen and it might just have to be the way we get rid of Phelan.

Ask yourself, "how many State Representatives and State Senators did nothing to protect our rights when Abbott crossed the line and violated his oath of office?" By not "protecting and defending the constitution," they violated their oaths as well and deserve the same fate. Long term we need to rotate out our public servants so they never take our votes for granted again. Once we elect a clean slate of conservative patriots, we can pass the legislative priorities that 60 to 70 percent of us support.

I would agree we are in a mess and we didn't get here overnight. The corruption has been going on for years but we don't have to stay in this mess.

We can always be working towards progress today and for future generations. If it isn't election season then we can use that time to grow in numbers, plan and organize. We can engage in person, on social platforms and push back when our kids in college start talking about what they have "learned" about capitalism of socialism.

Make It Happen Summary

✓ "What can I do," and how The Five Star Plan answers with real action.

✓ The importance of phone scripts and attending or holding meetings.

✓ Action is the key to success.

✓ Monitor our elected legislatures, never look away and never stop holding them accountable.

9

What The Elected Can Do

Anyone can run for office or you can get other people that you trust and respect to run for office. This is something you should remember when you're recruiting those five and pass that same advice along. It might take some sifting through but they are out there and now more than ever voters are paying close attention.

This idea that you have to be part of a club to run for office is how we ended up with these elite career politicians. No one on either side of the table is entitled to hold a certain office and at some point, the voter has forgotten that. We don't have to settle for the lesser of two evils. We can lead our communities and state back to, "Me Public, You Servant."

When elected to office, a Sheriff can refuse to enforce unconstitutional laws, or mandates. Judges can throw out cases where no laws were broken and rule as if the federal and state constitutions actually apply instead of treating laws as supreme to the constitutions.

County Commissioners can set the salary of an out of control county judge, they can even suspend their salary if they have a majority vote. County judges can also turn down the unconstitutional executive power that Abbott is offering. Our Texas State Representatives and Senators can publicly announce when a governor is acting unlawfully and even call their own special session in order to consider impeachment.

The Texas AG could sue the governor of Texas for changing election law without any input from lawmakers before suing the governors of other states for doing the exact same thing. Everyone should be holding the elected accountable because you are in charge of your actions. Let these people know what you want from them at every level and remind them an election is right around the corner. Make it clear you expect them to follow their oaths and not side with a tyrant.

Qualifications for elected office does vary and they can change. This information will always be available on the Secretary of State website. These requirements are not complex and it might surprise you to know that a Texas County Judge does not require a law degree, or any other type of degree. If you're willing to stay within the limits placed by the law and do the right thing, then you would do a far better job that most of Austin or D.C. in either party.

The point is, if you choose to be a candidate or find someone willing to run and you meet the requirements then you are eligible. You are more likely to do the right thing for the people than someone who has sold out to the establishment.

Leading our communities and state comes with the responsibility to serve the people and not the other way around.

What the Elected Can-Do Summary

✓ How we ended up with elite politicians.

✓ We don't have to settle for the lesser of two evils.

✓ Accountability as elected and to the voter.

✓ Leading the people with integrity.

10

What It Takes To Win

What it takes to win comes down to needing more votes than the other side. Sounds simple but if you are running in a race with 500 voters for a Precinct Chair verses millions of votes in a Governor's race, then you cannot waste time on those who will never or most likely not vote for you.

A good example would be if you were running for a Precinct Chair, you would not waste time visiting the opponent or their parents and family. You don't have to visit your supporter's homes, but you do need to spend all the time you can with the people that will be voting and could vote either way. Towards the end of the campaign it's also important to contact and ensure your supporters actually get to the polls. Professional politicians can spend millions planning out who, where, how and when to talk to people.

Since you are just starting out, getting the voter list for that office from the last election will help. That list can be gathered from the county or the state and it will show who voted and if they voted in the Republican or Democratic Primary and how often. They may also charge a small fee for this information.

If you have a lot of ground to cover and little time you might skip voters based on age or gender. If you are doing really well or really poorly with a given group, 50% plus one is the goal. Many people aim for a landslide and wind up failing. This is due to not spending enough time with the 51% and too much time with the 49% that were never going to vote for you or even vote at all.

Planning a complex campaign involves recruiting, budgeting, fundraising, information, establishing a team, targeting, paperwork, speeches, press releases, and social media. Putting together a team really won't be difficult if you've already begun recruiting for the five-star plan. It's also possible to find quality team members from your conservative/patriot group meetings that you've already been attending.

The theme is easy, focus on the constitution and standing up to anyone, in either party, that tries to violate the rights of the citizens. You will not outlaw businesses, nor place people under house arrest without a crime or a trial. You will not declare some people's job essential and others non-essential. You will not make it a crime to gather and worship. Sounds wild right? You rebel, you radical.

Recruiting is the key and it begins with talking to people, gathering those names and their contact information from now until 2022. Even if you don't run for office gather this information because if you find someone better you can turn these contacts over to that candidate running in your county or district. You can even reach out yourself and ask those contacts to support a particular candidate or a list of Texas Five-Star candidates. This list is essentially your own political party and they are trusting you to guide them.

WHAT IS YOUR TALENT & COMMITMENT?

Imagine you were a professional telemarketer and love to work the phones. Guess where you can do the most good? You know how to fundraise and have a contact list that is worth billions. Guess who shouldn't be knocking on doors but should be raising cash?

Your talents, what you are really good at and enjoy are what makes you unique and nobody else should be assigning you to tasks. Make a list of goals and use your talents to get them done. If you are even mildly interested in running for office please register and run because hardly anyone ever does.

Forming a County organization to support your candidates and your party is a good way to grow momentum. When my wife and I started the Arapahoe County Tea Party, we honestly had no idea what we were doing. We put up a free webpage that the group still uses and found a local coffee shop to meet monthly. When the group became too large, we used a community center at an apartment complex. When the State Tea Party of Colorado informed us, they never gave us permission to form I told them "Great, I never asked."

A month later we had more members than the rest of the state combined and the group still boasts several hundred members and can turn out upwards of a thousand at rallies and tens of thousands of phone calls in an election season.

Starting a county organization and having one or two meetings a month is doable. As long as you have a clear message and a goal, nothing is stopping you from attracting members. A clear calendar of activities is also important. You cannot have meeting after meeting where there is a speaker or it just turns into a complaint festival. This is where having goals and announcing your progress comes in. Accomplishments and growth bring forward excitement. This will attract new members and keep the original ones involved.

Keeping in touch is something I am horrible at because I get busy with work and in general lose track of months and years when it comes to people. This is not good when leading a group of people. Keep a planner handy so your making regular monthly calls to members you didn't see at the last meeting. They might have a good reason for being absent or have simply misunderstood something that was said. By reaching out you can find out if they are off your members list or want additional duties. You never want to bump into them a year later and find out they stopped attending because you never called.

"Oh, that was yesterday?" I should have a shirt that says this. I live in the moment is one way of saying it but "scatterbrained" is the term my wife uses. I have a lot going on and it gets jumbled. If I don't write something down, I will forget it more often than I can remember. Most people are the same way; if you start a group with a website don't forget to include a monthly schedule and include an email subscription. There are many companies providing email delivery like Mailerlite, Constant Contact, and Convert kit to name a few and they're not difficult to use.

I dislike asking for money so never put me in charge of fundraising. I have been "beans and rice broke" and I have been well off. I am generous when flush but would rather go hungry than ask for a meal. You'll notice there's no donation button on TFSP website. As a working stiff I will ask, "pass the hat" at small gatherings where I speak. My wife put her foot down on travel expenses when we head out to far away events. After all I'm already taking a day off work to attend. If you're like me and hate asking for money, find someone that is more comfortable with that assignment and put them in charge.

Put together a reading list. By looking up any topic online you can find books on almost any subject and we have recommendations on the website under resources. Reading and reading a lot is important. People say things in certain ways that you and I would have never thought of and using that as a guide can help improve and communicate ideas better than you could ever do on your own.

Many people feel they would do a better job in Austin or congress than the people we have now. Why don't they run? Is it because they don't know how? Not only do they not know how, they don't even know who to ask. Faced with that, they roll over and go back to sleep. The next time a person tells you they could do a better job find out why they haven't asked for the job. Find out when they plan on running and offer to help them track down the information and get elected. Sometimes all it takes is a little encouragement and the best people for office are often the ones that are humble.

Going back to the bible, "Ask and you shall...." You might have to ask more than once and you may have to just ask the right people. All the information on running for office is available and can be received. Remember the Secretary of State's website has almost everything you need. There are books with pronounced titles like "How to Win a State or Local Election." There are people in office you may respect, even if they're not your representative they could help. I know at least one woman in WA State that communicated with U.S. Senator Rand Paul to get her questions answered and he wasn't even in her time zone. In Texas, as I write this you might contact Col. Allen West, Chairman of the Republican Party. I would assume he would be able and willing to help or at least know the right people to ask.

In sales training you would be told to ask for the sale three times. When it comes to collecting information, never stop asking until you have it. A few examples could be the following.

- How to choose a speaker?
- What are Chinese drones?
- Where does the money comes from?
- Where do I find the list of candidates we like?
- What important dates I should know?
- When, where and how do I register people to vote?
- When, where and how do I register to run for office?

For people just getting involved there are several things to know. Before the General Election there are Primary Elections, remember this and write it down if you need to. There could be several Republicans and Democrats trying to win these primaries. This is the point where you can accept or reject the candidate that currently holds the seat without voting for "the other side." Once the primaries are over then you have a choice between the two parties. You know about the General and the Primary Elections but do you know about the "Special Elections?"

Special Elections take place when a current office holder can no longer hold that office. If a current office holder resigns, dies, or wins another office most often the state will hold a "Special Election." The reason these are important is because office holders who already have a staff and a campaign fund have a huge advantage. These elections can be as short as a week between the filing date and the start of early voting.

Many times, these office holders may win re-elections and then resign in order to "pick" their replacement. The person they choose will know when the office will come open and might already have a team together and campaign materials ready to go. Most of us will learn about the special election too late to actually be able to compete on an equal footing.

Imagine learning you can file on the first and that early voting will start on the 7th. You need to organize, get voter rolls, design campaign material, raise money and unless you already have a lot of that in place you cannot even get out of the gate before the election is over. I am not saying it's impossible but it is far more productive in most cases to remember how the person got the job and bide your time until the next primary.

You might still run just to get the word out and gain some name recognition but it will be a huge uphill struggle to win one of these special elections without a serious amount of backing.

Monitor and keep track of the candidates you helped and use the same standards as you apply to the opposition. Once you recruited a great candidate and they win their election, are you done? Absolutely Not because people change. People in public office tend to shift a lot quicker than we realize. They might learn they cannot get anything accomplished if they do not "play the game" and getting reelected might take priority over actually doing what they went there to do.

Keep an eye on these people and be ready to call them out when they start acting like the person they replaced.

What It Takes To Win Summary

✓ Planning your campaign, the theme and recruiting volunteers.

✓ What is your talent and commitment?

✓ Forming a county organization.

✓ What are Special Elections?

11

Where We Are At

So where are we at? We need to replace career politicians with patriots and we need to keep trading so one does not become the other. Politics was never intended to be a lifelong career any more than jury duty was intended to be a career.

Being an involved citizen does require effort, freedom is the reward. Freedom is worth the cost. I have served with people in the military that gave their lives but they are gone. They did their part, now it's time for you and I to do ours. We have to be willing to stand up and challenge people that care more about their "club" than our constitution.

We cannot depend on any candidate to do the job for us. Trump was a great President and might be again, but at 74 is it guaranteed he will be able to run in 2024?

There are many moving parts in our country. Texas by itself is massive but your precinct only contains about 500 voters. Have you spoken to any of them? Do you know who your Precinct Chair is or even know if you have one?

Your precinct, community, county and your state need your help. There is corruption, stupidity and arrogance at almost every level and you have very little say at the top. Your donations might be drowned out and your voice may be silenced at the state or national level. You must realize that all of this is balanced on the backs of each voter. The bottom of the ladder, your precinct, holds the rest of it off the ground.

Out of that 500 voters in your precinct, is the best Republican sitting in that position right now? If not, do you have a better option? Then start by knocking on doors and getting that better person the votes needed to replace the present seat holder. While you're sharing the word, you might be surprised to find like-minded individuals willing to help you out.

Once your precinct is taken care of look at your Republican County Chair. Attend a meeting, ask questions and find out if they're doing that job for the good of the community or for some other reason.

Find out if surrounding Precinct Chairs need to be filled or replaced. Nothing says you cannot knock doors a few blocks over; this is also a great way to meet people. Find out if they want to join together to make things better and find out if they would consider running for office. If you don't ask you might never know.

In many of the Texas counties I've travelled, I have been told about the layers of corruption that exists. If you know about such things it is your duty to report it. If it is a rumor you could track it down. If enough private citizens called the State Attorney General's office about a particular topic it would get attention. Choose to do nothing and the corruption grows.

Contacting your State Representative is the next step up on the ladder. Many elected to these positions have done nothing but break the rules of the party and their oath by not defending the constitution. Many endorse horrible candidates that even you or I would have a good chance of beating in the Primary Election.

When it comes to our State Senators or U.S. Congress, this is where you have to get serious about building your groups and networking with other counties. In Texas, a state senator actually represents more people than a congressman. These races can spend into the millions on ads, signs and materials.

You should remember that a bad incumbent can face censure by Republican County Chairs, that you help put in place. Don't forget about all those fine city and county officials you helped get elected because you can ask them to endorse Five-Star candidates. Winning a race where every elected official is on your side and the opponent has been censured for a specific reason adds momentum to your chances of winning.

We have covered elected offices from Precinct to U.S. Congress and fixing this mess will not be quick or easy. There will be victories and defeats. Even if we lose, every race will teach us something new and we'll learn where to improve for next time. These lessons may be centered around where to spend time and money or they might mean you need to double the size of your group before the next election season.

Every year when you engage in activity you will meet new people, grow closer to people from those previous years and find new ways to move forward. You will get younger and older people involved and in time these efforts will get results. We always hope they will get results right away but we did not get where we are overnight and we will not fix everything at once.

Don't get down, Douglas MacArthur said, "All courage is based in optimism." I find these words to ring true. No one wants to engage in an activity that does not matter. The men at the Alamo thought that perhaps reinforcements would arrive if they held out a little longer. They thought if they could delay Santa Anna long enough for Sam Houston to put together an army their cause would win even if they died. This is optimism.

YOU are reading this; YOU are the one that wants to make a difference and YOU are the one we are all counting on. Find others like you and build a group.

Honor those that came before us with your actions. Build something better for the ones that come after us with your actions.

There are people that look at politics as they would a sports team. They root for their players no matter what and only pay attention during elections. There are also people that make it their identity and stay active year-round for more of the "look at me" instead of making things better.

At the national level poor policy on national defense and immigration can cost lives. At the state level the criminal justice system, disaster response and infrastructure can kill people just as quickly.

When Hurricane Katrina hit New Orleans did is shock you to know there was no evacuation plan except for the political leaders themselves? If you or I were to be elected mayor of a city located beneath sea level on the Gulf Coast would it not be our first priority to plan an emergency response to protect the people that gave us that job?

In many cases professional politicians are too concerned with their next job, next election or next campaign contribution to have any real concern for our health and wellbeing. Unresponsive politicians lead to the deaths of people every day across this nation and unconcerned voters share in that responsibility by reelecting them. We never know when the next disaster will strike or what it will look like. We do know that politicians and bureaucrats will tell us all is well before it happens, fail us while it happens and blame others after it happens. Sometimes, if enough people die, they will try to solve it but they will always ask you to give up more freedoms and more tax dollars to fix things. Things that would have never been broken if they had stayed out of it in the first place or listened when they were warned.

This book is my attempt to provide people with the information and motivation to get us back to our heritage of a free and independent people without a professional political elite. Patriots that know how to care and represent the voter instead of fulltime fundraisers that seek to live at our expense while pretending to be our masters.

I hope this journey towards trading politicians for patriots is well underway before the next disaster hits and incompetence kills but my experience tells me it will not.

Voting is not where your involvement ends, it is where it begins. Get started now.

Acknowledgements

First off, I wish to thank all the people who asked me. "What can we do?"

Without all of these people who wanted to make a difference and didn't know where to start, this book would have never even been a goal, let alone a reality.

To my best friend, editor and my wife who all happen to be the same person, thank you Carole.

Next up I would like to thank Rick Parent for the cover photo of this book. In fact, everyone should thank Rick. If not for him my face may have ended up on the cover and trust me the Texas Flag is far easier on the eyes.

To the generous people that donated their time to write the reviews. Thank you so much for all that you do, have done and will continue to do in the future.

About Author

Robert West is a Native Texas Veteran. He met his wife Carole while serving in the U.S. Navy and they have two grown children. For 30 years, he's been working in avionics across the U.S. and overseas. He solves complex problems then heads home where he develops land part-time.

He's an advocate for small government and a true fiscal conservative. With strong conservative values Robert's been active in politics since founding one of the largest U.S. Tea Party groups. He currently serves as a Republican Precinct Chair in Delta County and like you, he's tired of career politicians. At various functions and events, he's often asked, "What can I do?"

People want to be involved but they don't know what steps to take. This led him to writing, The Five Star Plan and traveling around Texas sharing this message. Robert is focused on helping put Texas voters back in charge.

GET MORE CONTENT

TFSP BLOG
FREE RESOURCES

State Links
Printable Flyers
Five Star Legislatures
Political Groups

SPEAKING

Book Robert for your Group

THEFIVESTARPLAN.COM

Book Reviews

Robert West's book, "The Five Star Plan" lays out in clear, specific detail how "we the people" can regain our role in ensuring that our founding fathers' brilliant plan for life, liberty and individual pursuit of happiness can be rescued from the dominating hand of the socialist democrats who now control too many states and our nation. "The Five Star Plan" is a must read for every constitutional conservative with Judeo- Christian values.

Texas Senator, Bob Hall

The Five Star Plan is a roadmap to the possible restoration of the Republican Party. A great vision for the future of the Republican Party is laid out in an easy to understand manner. The Five Star Plan is an excellent read.

Tracy Jones

The Five Star Plan by Robert West is the quintessential "How to" for citizens who are ready to take their first steps toward political action. This book maps the political course for anyone who's fed up with the current status of our nation, state and local governments and has the desire to implement change. No stone is left unturned and excuses of political ignorance are extinguished. This is a must read for new and veteran activists.

Shelley Luther

The Five Star Plan is a great resource for the nuts and bolts of Texas Politics from the ground up. In addition, also a great tool to help Republicans grow their support, educate their base and win new people to our cause.

Texas Representative, Bryan Slaton

"The price of liberty is eternal vigilance."

Thomas Jefferson

Made in the USA
Columbia, SC
08 October 2021

46489122R00083